Mysteries
OF THE
SUPERNATURAL

© Aladdin Books Ltd 1996

Designed and produced by
Aladdin Books Ltd
28 Percy Street
London W1P 0LD

First published in the United States in 1996 by
Copper Beech Books,
an imprint of The Millbrook Press
2 Old New Milford Road
Brookfield, Connecticut

Editor: Katie Roden
Design:
David West Children's Book Design
Designer: Edward Simkins
Picture Research: Brooks Krikler Research
Illustrators: Francis Phillipps and Rob Shone

Printed in Belgium

Library of Congress Cataloging-in-Publication Data
Powell, Jillian.
The supernatural / by Jillian Powell: illustrated by Francis Phillipps and Rob Shone.
p. cm. -- (Mysteries of--)
Includes index.
Summary: Explores numerous mysterious places and powers,
UFOs and aliens, ghosts and the spirit world, mysterious creatures and people,
and mysteries solved and unsolved.
ISBN 0-7613-0455-X (lib. bdg.). --
ISBN 0-7613-0470-3
1. Parapsychology--Juvenile literature. 2. Supernatural--Juvenile literature.
[1. Parapsychology. 2. Supernatural. 3. Ghosts.]
I. Francis Phillipps and Rob Shone, ill. II. Title. III. Series.
BF1031.P75244 1996
133--dc20   95-40837
                               CIP
                               AC

Mysteries
OF THE
SUPERNATURAL

Jillian Powell

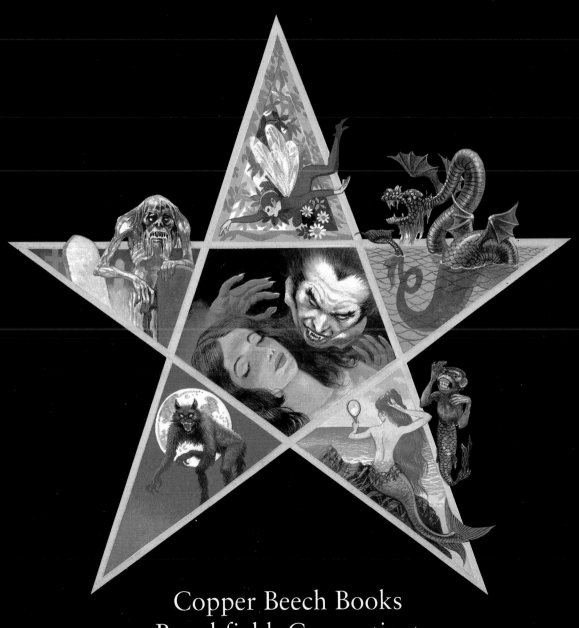

Copper Beech Books
Brookfield, Connecticut

CONTENTS

"We stand on...new frontiers of discovery which will test [our] courage and [our] ability to adapt."

Tim Dinsdale, Loch Ness Monster hunter

Introduction to
THE MYSTERIES

Since the earliest times, people have feared and wondered at the supernatural. The Stone Age paintings of animals in European caves were probably intended to have magical powers. As they painted bison and mammoths, early peoples believed they were calling up spirits to help them in their hunting. Cave painting was a way of bringing fertility or plenty, just as later peoples used dancing and rituals to bring rain or a good harvest, believing that unknown forces controlled human fortunes. In many cultures, gifts were offered to the gods or ancestors, to keep them happy.

Belief in monsters, spirits, and gods has become part of folklore and mythology, but the supernatural is still part of our lives. Newspapers carry horoscopes for people who think their lives are influenced by the movements of the stars. Mediums and hypnotists perform to packed audiences. Interest in new forms of health care, such as crystals and faith healing, has never been stronger. Science and technology bring us new discoveries about our world and the universe every day, but we are still fascinated by the mysteries of the supernatural.

The Early MYSTERIES

> "The mysterious monument of Stonehenge, standing remote on a bare and boundless heath, as much unconnected with the events of past ages as it is with the uses of the present, carries you back beyond all historical record into the obscurity of a totally unknown period."
>
> John Constable, British painter (1776–1837)

Stonehenge, in southern England, has remained a mystery for centuries. Who built this huge stone circle on Salisbury Plain, carrying stones over 19 feet (6 m) tall and weighing up to 50 tons, from the Welsh mountains? How did they have the mathematical knowledge and engineering skills to design and build it?

According to an early legend, the stone circle was created by the wizard Merlin. In the 1960s, the writer Erich von Däniken claimed it was built by aliens. Many attempts have been made to explain the monument. Recent archaeology shows it was probably begun in about 2800 B.C. and built in three stages over 1,500 years. Scientists have discovered that many of its arches and angles are lined up with important positions of the Sun and the Moon. Could the circle have been a vast stone computer, enabling early people to predict astronomical events? Perhaps we will never explain the mystery of Stonehenge.

Spooky PLACES

Stonehenge is only one of many mysterious places. Ancient sites often seem to attract supernatural events, such as sightings of ghosts and aliens. One theory is that standing stones and earthworks (banks of earth built by early peoples) were placed at the crossing points of the magnetic energy lines that cross the Earth, to form a bridge to the sky. *Ley lines* are a network of straight lines which seem to link sites such as standing stones and barrows (mounds of earth covering graves) with holy places. Ancient trackways follow these lines; some scientists believe that they match the lines of force around the Earth's surface.

THE VANISHING CREW
On a calm afternoon in December 1872, the Mary Celeste was seen drifting in the Atlantic Ocean. Her log ended on November 25. The entire crew had vanished. Had they been attacked by a giant octopus, sucked into a whirlpool, abducted by aliens...or simply drowned?

MYSTERIOUS MONUMENTS
On the slopes of Easter Island, in the Pacific Ocean, stand dozens of giant stone statues. They were probably made in A.D. 1000–1500, in the quarries of the extinct volcano Rano Raruku. They are believed to represent spirits of ancestors, who magically protected the islanders.

Bermuda

Florida

Puerto Rico

DEADLY TRIANGLE
Off the coast of Florida is an area known as the Bermuda Triangle, where over 200 ships and planes have vanished mysteriously. Some disappearances can be explained as the result of unusual weather, but the rest are a puzzle. Many people think that there could be strange energies at work there.

What was Stonehenge used for?
Scientists believe that this great monument was a tribal gathering place and religious center, although no one can be sure. It is thought that the layout of the stones was used to predict important astronomical events. Tribal ceremonies were probably held there at certain times of the year.

PICTURES IN THE SAND

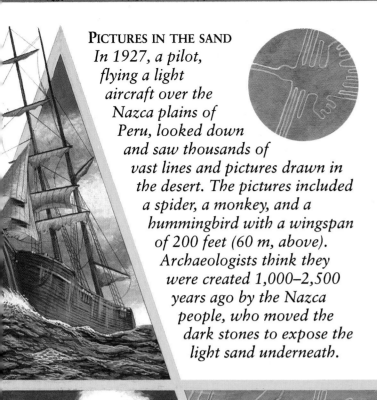

In 1927, a pilot, flying a light aircraft over the Nazca plains of Peru, looked down and saw thousands of vast lines and pictures drawn in the desert. The pictures included a spider, a monkey, and a hummingbird with a wingspan of 200 feet (60 m, above). Archaeologists think they were created 1,000–2,500 years ago by the Nazca people, who moved the dark stones to expose the light sand underneath.

Visitors from the skies

In 1969, Erich von Däniken wrote a book called *Chariots of the Gods?*, in which he suggested that aliens had visited Earth 10,000 years ago.

He claimed that they came from an advanced civilization and created many ancient wonders, like the Easter Island statues and Stonehenge. He said that some South American carvings (above) and a cave painting in Australia's Kimberley Mountains were images of alien visitors. Von Däniken said that early peoples worshiped the aliens and that many ancient myths were reports of their arrival in fiery chariots or spaceships.

POWERFUL STONES

The standing stones at Carnac, France are just one ancient site apparently chosen to match the Earth's energy lines. Thousands of huge stones are arranged in parallel rows, but no one knows why.

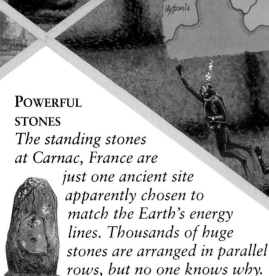

THE LOST CONTINENT

The ancient Greek philosopher Plato described a vast continent in the Atlantic known as Atlantis, which suddenly vanished. Huge undersea walls, from about 9500 B.C., have been found in the Bahamas. Could these have been the walls of Atlantis? Or did the legend arise from the flooding of the island of Crete in 1950 B.C.?

Strange
POWERS

To ancient peoples, natural disasters, such as earthquakes and volcanic eruptions, seemed like supernatural happenings. They watched the skies in awe, seeing comets as bloodthirsty serpents predicting doom and death. Even thunder and lightning seemed like warnings from the gods. Advanced technology now allows us to understand strange phenomena, but some ancient beliefs remain. When we read our horoscopes, we use the ancient art of astrology, believing that the movements of the stars affect our lives, while the use of "lucky" mascots shows that we still believe in the power of the supernatural.

MAGICAL GOLD
Medieval alchemists claimed to be able to turn ordinary metals into gold. They also tried to find the "elixir of life" – a tonic to cure all illnesses. Most of them were frauds, but their work helped chemical science to develop.

EVERY HAND TELLS A STORY
The art of palm reading has existed for centuries. Palmists "read" the lines on people's hands to see into their future. The left hand is said to show what they are born with and the right shows what they have become.

SPELL-MAKERS
Magical people are found worldwide. All are seen as able to affect nature and people's lives. After A.D. 900, the Christian church condemned magic. Many women were accused of witchcraft and killed. One test for a witch involved dunking the woman in water. If she floated, she was declared a witch and put to death. If she sank and drowned, she was proclaimed innocent!

LOOK OUT!
Some ancient beliefs claim that certain people can harm others by sight. In some cultures, images of eyes are worn, to protect against this "evil eye," by turning the evil back to where it came from.

A Dogon myth

The Dogon people of West Africa tell an ancient myth that long ago they were visited by aliens from Sirius (right), the brightest star. The aliens told them that the star had two companion stars, one of which orbited (traveled around) it every 50 years. In 1862, scientists found Sirius B, a small star that takes 50 years to orbit Sirius. How did the Dogon know this, so long before modern science?

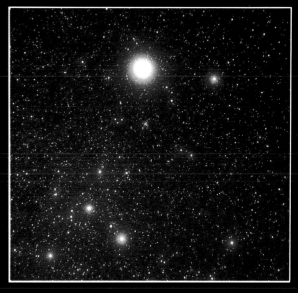

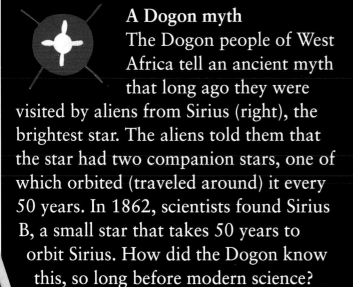

THE SCREAMING PLANT

It has long been believed that many plants are magical and can influence human lives. In medieval times, the root of the mandrake plant was thought to contain a demon, because of its forked, human-like shape. The root was said to give such a terrible scream when it was dug out of the ground that it could drive people mad, so dogs were used to pull mandrake roots up instead.

MYSTICAL CHARMS

Magic spells and charms have been used for thousands of years. Talismans are objects or figures used for witchcraft or voodoo (worship of tribal spirits). The earliest date from about 30,000 B.C. Many people believe in the power of crystals. Crystal balls are used by fortune-tellers, who claim to reveal the future.

When did people first use magic?
The first evidence of magic dates from about 50,000 B.C., when early peoples buried bears as part of magic rituals. Many cave paintings may have been done for magic purposes – to bring success to hunters, for example. The ancient Egyptians also used a variety of magic objects, while legend says that the biblical Three Kings found Jesus by astrological use of the stars.

Secrets of the S K I E S

For many centuries, people have been fascinated by strange lights and objects in the sky. Some of the first descriptions of UFOs (Unidentified Flying Objects) were made by the ancient Greeks and Romans, who reported "phantom chariots" speeding across the heavens.

Until the Industrial Revolution (a period of scientific progress in the 19th century), sightings were interpreted as signs from heaven to warn of disasters. Ufology (the study of UFOs) developed after World War II, when space travel became possible and there were fears of invasion. There have since been regular UFO sightings around the world. Some ufologists believe that UFOs are alien spacecraft, visiting Earth to study humans and take back samples. Many people claim to have been kidnapped by aliens. Early myths told of abductions by gods, monsters, and fairies, while modern witnesses describe "little green men" and high-tech spacecraft.

UFOs and ALIENS

40 million UFO sightings have been recorded since 1947, when the first "flying saucers" were reported. The most common sightings are of glowing balls of light, moving quickly. There have been reports of crash landings by mysterious objects and of alien abductions. In 1948, the U.S. Air Force set up an investigation into UFOs. By 1969, when the project ended, about 12,000 incidents had been recorded. A quarter were caused by natural phenomena or known objects, but the rest remained unidentified. It has yet to be proved that there are intelligent life forms elsewhere in space – or that they are visiting Earth.

KIDNAPPED!
People who claim to have been abducted by aliens often describe strange noises, flashing lights, and blackouts. Some say they were examined, losing hair and fingernails, and developing strange marks on their skin.

TIME TRAVELERS
No other planet in our solar system can support life, so UFOs must come from planets orbiting another star like our Sun. It would take thousands of years to reach us from the nearest star. Some people think that aliens can "beam" their ships across space and time.

MYSTERY AT ROSWELL
In 1995, British ufologists unveiled an old film showing U.S. scientists examining the corpse of an alien (below). It has been linked to a reported UFO crash near Roswell, NM, in 1947. The U.S. government claimed the wreckage was a weather balloon, but others said they were hiding a "spy" balloon...or a UFO. The film is now being tested – perhaps the truth will be known at last.

Where do UFOs come from?
Most ufologists believe that aliens visit Earth from distant galaxies which human science and technology are not yet advanced enough to find. However, some people have a theory that UFOs come from a hollow area in the center of the Earth and fly into space through a hole at the North Pole!

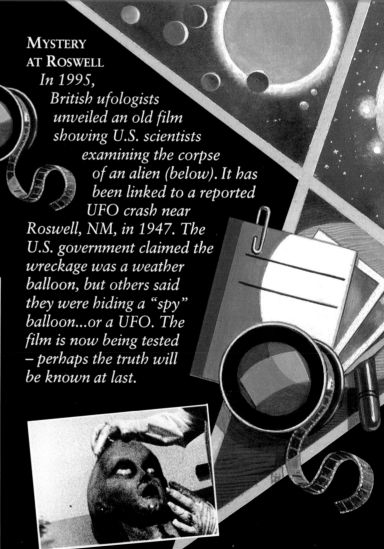

CLOSE ENCOUNTERS

UFO sightings are called Close Encounters. *A* Close Encounter *of the First Kind is seeing a UFO. The* Second Kind *includes evidence such as landing marks. The* Third Kind *is when a witness sees or meets alien beings. In 1947, a pilot saw some strange disks in the sky. He told reporters that they looked like "saucers" and the name "flying saucers" caught on.*

FACING THE ALIENS

UFOs appear in many shapes and sizes! On April 24, 1964, a police officer claimed that he saw an egg-shaped craft land and two small, human-like creatures climb out. The aliens saw him, rushed back to the ship, and took off. Scorch marks were later found where the ship had been standing.

Tracking alien beings

Everyone has seen imaginary UFOs in films such as *Close Encounters of the Third Kind* (below), but ufologists investigate UFO sightings by real-life witnesses. They use hi-tech equipment to measure radio waves and magnetic effects which might be caused by UFOs, and track mysterious craft on radar screens. Amateur ufologists watch the skies using telescopes and cameras. If they spot a UFO, they record its position, movement, color, and shape, and send this data to UFO organizations. Permanent observers now keep watch for UFOs around the world.

ENCOUNTER OVER IRAN

On September 9, 1976, a UFO was seen over Iran. Two planes went to investigate, but their controls jammed. The UFO, which was about 160 feet long, seemed to fire at them before speeding away.

Tricks and
IMAGINATION

In the 20th century, UFOs and aliens have become a familiar part of our culture. Many science fiction books are bestsellers, films like *E.T.*, *Close Encounters of the Third Kind*, *Alien*, and *Star Trek* attract enormous audiences, and organizations have been set up around the world to record and investigate UFO sightings. This fascination has led to some clever hoaxes. Many fake photographs of UFOs have been made by photographing miniature models in close-up, or by tampering with photographic negatives. Some people have faked UFO sightings and evidence of landings by spacecraft. There have even been suggestions that extraterrestrials are already living in secret on Earth...and a few people have claimed to be aliens!

THE REAL UFOs
During World War II, U.S. pilots reported seeing fiery balls in the sky, which they nicknamed "foo fighters." They were thought to be natural phenomena or UFOs. In fact, the Germans had developed disk-shaped anti-radar craft. The fuel caused a fiery "halo." Since then, Russia and the U.S. may have created a disk-shaped supersonic craft, using UFO reports as a cover-up.

STRANGE SIGHTS IN OUTER SPACE
Many reports of moving lights in the sky are often found later to be sightings of falling meteors or comets. Venus, the brightest planet in the night sky, is clearly visible with the naked eye and has frequently been mistaken for a UFO.

SKY LIGHTS
Ball lightning has scared people for centuries. It appears as a red, yellow, orange, or green fiery ball and is seen during storms, usually after ordinary lightning. No one knows why it occurs.

Fake photographs

A photograph of a UFO, apparently taken by an airline pilot over Venezuela in 1965, was believed to be genuine until 1971. A U.S. photographic expert pointed out that the UFO was too sharply outlined to be a distant object and could not have created the shadow underneath it. The "UFO" was a button, placed over a picture of the sky and re-photographed. The shadow had been chemically burned in during the processing of the film. This is one of the most convincing UFO fakes ever, but there have been many more since then!

NATURAL UFOs

Horizontal formations of cloud can look saucer-like, especially when light shines on them. Unusual weather conditions can cause strange signals on radar screens, which may be mistaken for UFOs.

NEW THEORIES

A report has suggested a link between alien stories and the drama of birth. Aliens are usually described as having big heads and short limbs, like babies. Do tales of bright tunnels resemble a baby's experience of being born?

THE CROWDED SKIES

All kinds of flying objects have been mistaken for UFOs over the years, including planes, airships, weather balloons, satellites, kites, and even flocks of birds.

How are movie UFOs created?
For many years, special effects teams have used small models to create UFO effects. The models are photographed in a series of pictures which, when played back at high speed, give the illusion of movement. Recently, hi-tech computer programs have made it possible to achieve even more spectacular extraterrestrial action, allowing animators to move and manipulate all kinds of images.

Mysteries of the SPIRIT WORLD

> "All houses in which men have
> lived and died
> Are haunted houses: through the
> open doors
> The harmless phantoms on their
> errands glide
> With feet that make no sound
> upon the floors."
>
> Henry Wadsworth Longfellow,
> American poet and critic
> (1807–1882)

Belief in ghosts and spirits is found in every culture. Stone Age peoples (before about 10,000 B.C.) buried bodies weighted down with stones or with their hands and feet tied together, so their ghosts would not be able to rise up and wander. In Africa, China, Japan, South America, and other areas, people feared the return of their dead ancestors and performed special rituals to please their spirits.

For many years, people have believed that ghosts are trapped between this world and the next. They may be paying for a wrong they committed when alive, or visiting this world to give a message or warning. Parapsychologists (people who study supernatural human powers) say that ghosts are created by energy released by our minds, leaving an imprint which some people can see. Others think that ghosts are caused by telepathy between the living and the dead, but some say this is all made-up nonsense. Do *you* believe in ghosts?

Ghosts and POLTERGEISTS

White ladies, screaming skulls, moaning monks, and spooky dogs – all appear in stories of ghosts told throughout the ages. There have been many sightings of ghost ships, believed to bring bad luck. Witnesses of ghosts describe strange noises, like knocking or crying, and there may be an unusual smell or a drop in temperature. Ghosts are often seen to wear old-fashioned clothes or white robes (perhaps the shrouds in which they were buried) and are usually attached to a certain house or place. They can pass through walls and climb invisible stairs, as if following the routes they knew when alive. People have seen them in churches, cemeteries, and even in airports and on highways.

Do ghosts usually haunt graveyards?
Most ghosts haunt the place where they died, so it is unusual to find them in graveyards at all! But graveyards are said to be guarded by the ghost of the first person buried there. In Western Europe, early peoples buried human sacrifices at new burial grounds, to act as guardians.

THE FIRST GHOST?
The first known record of a ghost appears in an ancient Babylonian tale, The Epic of Gilgamesh, *dating from 2300–2100 B.C. The story, pictured on clay tablets, shows how a friend of King Gilgamesh (left) of Sumeria (now southeastern Iraq) appeared to him as a transparent ghost.*

DEMON CREATURES
There are many accounts of phantom dogs, bringing bad luck to those who saw them. "Black Shuck" (right) was said to be as big as a calf, with a black coat and one eye. Such stories may have been inspired by dogs with the disease rabies, which causes madness.

GHOST DANCING
In the late 19th century, many Native North American peoples performed ghost dances, asking the spirits of their animal ancestors to help them drive European settlers from their lands. Special costumes were worn, with a different design for each ancestor. People also danced to contact their personal animal spirits. Such dances are still performed today in some areas.

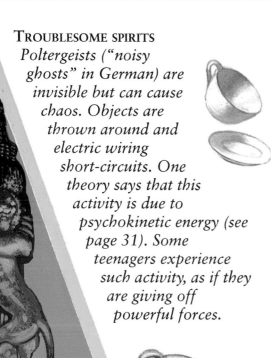

TROUBLESOME SPIRITS
Poltergeists ("noisy ghosts" in German) are invisible but can cause chaos. Objects are thrown around and electric wiring short-circuits. One theory says that this activity is due to psychokinetic energy (see page 31). Some teenagers experience such activity, as if they are giving off powerful forces.

A GHOST'S BEST FRIEND
Dogs and cats may show distress in places thought to be haunted. Can they see or sense something which we cannot? Scientists think they might be sensitive to increased electricity in the air, which does not affect humans.

Haunted houses
Old houses are often believed to be haunted. The ghost may be the restless spirit of someone who lived or died in the house. Borley Rectory in England (below) was said to be the most haunted house in the world. A headless man and phantom coach were seen, strange noises were heard, and mysterious graffiti appeared on the walls. It was destroyed by fire in 1939, but reports of hauntings continue in nearby Borley Church. The Drury Lane Theater, in London, is said to be haunted by a man whose skeleton was found in the wall.

GHOST TALK
A séance is a group of people who hope to make contact with the dead, led by a medium, one who claims to speak to spirits. Messages are spelled out on a Ouija board (right).

Phantoms...or FAKES?

On a dark night, it is easy to imagine strange noises or shapes in the shadows, but some "ghostly" sounds are just creaking floorboards, scuffling mice, or heating pipes expanding! For centuries, people reported seeing giant, ghostly figures in the Harz Mountains in Germany. In the 19th century, it was realized that when the Sun set, climbers cast shadows, up to 650 feet (200 m) tall, onto the clouds around the peaks of the mountains.

Researchers now investigate spirit sightings and activity with infrared cameras and hi-tech instruments which detect drafts, vibrations, and temperature changes. They must rule out any natural phenomena which could offer explanations for ghosts, as well as hoaxes and fakes.

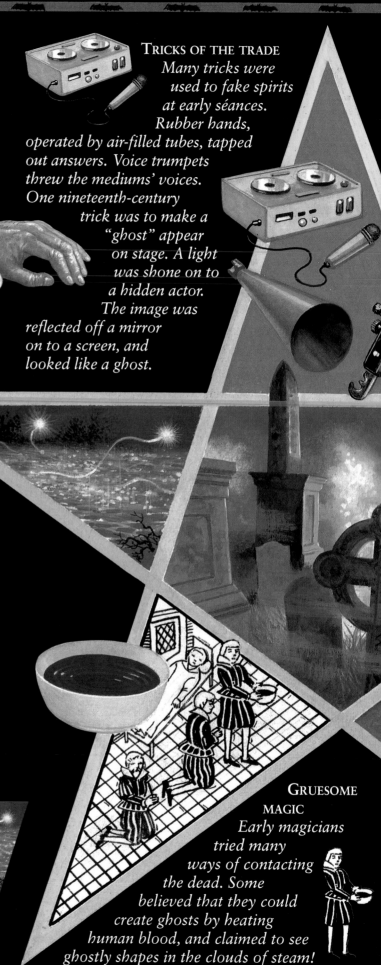

WILL O' THE WISP
Marsh lights are moving flames seen at night on marshy land. They are caused by smoky gases released from rotting vegetation. They were once known as "Will o' the Wisps" or "Jack o' Lanterns" and were thought to be the ghosts of children who lured travelers into bogs and quicksand.

GRUESOME MAGIC
Early magicians tried many ways of contacting the dead. Some believed that they could create ghosts by heating human blood, and claimed to see ghostly shapes in the clouds of steam!

Say "Cheese!"

Spirit photography became a craze in the 19th century. Photographers faked pictures by developing "ghostly" images of models on the same pictures as portraits of real people. Some spirit photographs are less easily explained, like the picture of a ghostly monk standing by the altar rail in Newby Abbey, Yorkshire, England (see pages 4–5). The priest who took the picture, in the 1960s, said that the ghost appeared when the film was developed. Experts can find no evidence of forgery.

SECRET GHOSTS

Eighteenth-century smugglers made use of superstitions. One painted his horses white, except for their heads, and fixed lights to his coach. At night, witnesses saw headless horses and a ghostly carriage!

GHOSTBUSTERS

Researchers use hi-tech equipment, but fake ghosts are caught by using powder to reveal footprints or by tying thread over doors to see if they are opened – real ghosts would walk right through them!

DEADLY LIGHTS

When people first saw tiny flames in graveyards, in the 1960s, they thought they were ghosts, showing the way a funeral procession would pass. These "corpse lights" were probably gases seeping through the soil from rotting plants or from bodies in shallow graves.

What is a ghost town?

Ghost towns aren't full of ghouls and spirits! In the 19th century, thousands of people rushed to remote areas of Australia and North America in search of gold, and founded towns near the mines. Once the mines were empty, the miners moved on, leaving the towns abandoned – "ghost towns."

"Humanity's knowledge of natural history was low in fact and high in fancy for so long that it is a daunting task now to separate the one from the other in legends and the older records."

Henry H. Bauer, author of *The Enigma of Loch Ness*, 1991

Incredible
BEINGS

Loch Ness is one of the largest lakes in Britain, 24 miles (39 km) long and 990 feet (300 m) deep. Its dark, peaty waters are often covered by mist, and it is easy to imagine that a strange monster might lurk in its mysterious underwater caves and tunnels.

There have been thousands of sightings of "Nessie" since the first recorded one in A.D. 565. A photo of a long-necked creature was taken by a doctor in 1934. It was recently proved to be a picture of a clockwork model, but many people still believe in the monster. Scientists have used modern technology, such as submarines, sonar, and underwater cameras, to examine the lake. Sonar signals have indicated a creature bigger than any of the fish known to be there. Some people believe that "Nessie" has survived from a prehistoric species, trapped in the lake since the Ice Age. Like the other strange creatures reported worldwide, the monster links myth and science, stretching everyone's imagination.

Supernatural CREATURES

Before people understood natural phenomena, they were thought to be caused by monsters. Without scientific knowledge, it was easy to imagine that a volcano belching smoke could be an evil demon, or that an electrical storm was sent by angry gods. Comets were seen as serpents of the sky, while in ancient China, dragons were believed to control the weather and the harvest. In the Middle East, sandstorms were thought to be caused by the *Jinn*, a demon. Most of the world has been explored, but wildernesses remain, in lakes, oceans, forests, and on remote mountains. It is here that unidentified creatures may lurk.

What is a monster?
The word "monster" comes from the Latin term *monstrum*, meaning an omen (warning). Ancient peoples thought that if they saw unusual creatures, or if animals behaved strangely, disaster was approaching. For example, the Mesopotamians believed that the king's palace would catch fire if a dog lay on his throne.

FAIRIES OR FAKES?
In 1917, two English girls produced photographs of fairies, which were declared genuine by experts. In 1978, a researcher saw the same "fairies" in a book from 1915. The girls had painted the fairies on cardboard then photographed them.

THE LIVING DEAD
There are many tales of people being turned into zombies. They come back from the dead, but nothing can stop them and they have no feelings. The zombie myth might have its roots in the trance states encouraged by religions such as voodoo, often caused by drugs.

THE BEAST WITHIN
Werewolves are said to be people who suddenly turn into wolf creatures at night, especially when the moon is full. They roam the land, looking for victims and feeding on their flesh. In the past, people suspected of being werewolves were tortured and burned. Some may have suffered from the illness lycanthropy ("moon madness"), whose victims think they are wild beasts, especially at full moon; or they may have gone mad after a bite from a dog with rabies.

SEA MONSTERS

Many unidentified creatures must still live in the dark ocean depths. Over the centuries, there have been thousands of sightings of sea monsters. They may often be explained as giant squid or octopuses, or terrifying sea serpents up to 99 feet (30 m) long.

The snow-dwellers

In 1921, the first explorers of Mount Everest were climbing through a pass, when they saw a group of hairy, apelike beasts. The guides said that they were *Yeti*, or "snow creatures," giving rise to the name "Abominable Snowmen." They were described as tall, with pointed heads and big hands and feet. There have been many sightings, but no one has ever caught or photographed a Yeti. The Sasquatch, also known as "Big Foot," is a human-like beast said to live in North American forests. Witnesses say that it cannot be stopped and can vanish suddenly.

SPIRITS OF THE SEA

Tales of mermaids have been popular since ancient times. In 1842, the "Feejee Mermaid" became the star of Phineas T. Barnum's traveling show. In fact, it was made from a monkey's body and a stuffed fish's tail!

BLOOD SUCKERS

Vampire tales began in medieval Europe. Some plague victims were buried before they had died. If they were dug up, they had bloody hands from trying to escape and were said to be vampires. The myth has lived on in books and movies (right).

Powerful PEOPLE

Every culture has beliefs about people with special powers, such as mediums, clairvoyants, faith healers, witch doctors, and soothsayers. Supernatural abilities have been viewed very differently over the centuries. The powers we now call psychokinetic energy and faith healing may in earlier times have been regarded as magic, sorcery, or witchcraft. Parapsychology is the modern scientific term for research into the mysterious powers which some people claim or are believed to have. We still do not know how these powers work, or how many people have them.

HEALING HANDS
Faith healers practice the art of healing without conventional surgery or medicines. Some claim to cure people by touching the patient. It is believed that healing energy passes between the healer and the patient. Other people say that the patient's recovery is due to his or her mind. He or she believes in the cure, so feels better.

LE MAT

SEEING INTO THE UNKNOWN
Clairvoyants claim to see things, people, or events in the future. For centuries, prophets and fortune-tellers have made use of such powers, either in trances or by "reading" objects like crystal balls. The Tarot (above) is a set of 78 cards used to foretell the future. It was probably first used in ancient Egypt, and includes cards like The Wheel of Fortune, Death, and The Devil.

HIDDEN ENERGY
Dowsing is the ancient art of finding water and minerals using a forked stick or dowsing rod. When certain substances are nearby, the rod twitches or bends. Modern dowsers may be employed to find underground pipes, cables, streams, and mineral deposits.

MEDICAL MAGIC

Witch doctors are important in tribal societies. They are thought to have the power to cure or cause diseases using herbs, spells, or curses. One explanation is that a person who believes in a spell will become ill or get better due to the power of the mind to affect the body.

A MOVING EXPERIENCE

Psychokinesis (PK), shown by some psychics, is the power to make objects move or bend by thought alone. The right side of the brain may hold such powers, which we have not learned to use or have forgotten about.

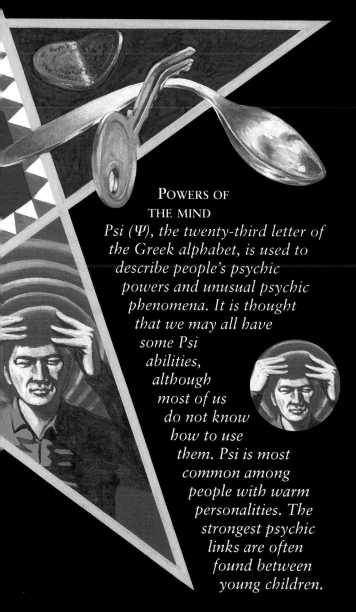

POWERS OF THE MIND

Psi (Ψ), the twenty-third letter of the Greek alphabet, is used to describe people's psychic powers and unusual psychic phenomena. It is thought that we may all have some Psi abilities, although most of us do not know how to use them. Psi is most common among people with warm personalities. The strongest psychic links are often found between young children.

A most mysterious man

Uri Geller became famous in the 1970s for his ability to bend metal by concentrating on it and stroking it. Spoons, forks, and keys continued to bend even after he had left the room! He also appeared to be able to stop engines and repair broken watches just by thought. Geller first became aware of these powers of psychokinesis (PK), when he was only four. Since 1985, he has used his powers to find underground oil and other minerals.

Do people's strange powers have any uses? Russian and U.S. scientists have been experimenting with Psi and extra-sensory perception (ESP, or communicating by thought alone) as a way of talking to submarines under polar ice, where they are out of the range of radios. Some police investigations have made use of psychics.

Mysteries Solved & UNSOLVED

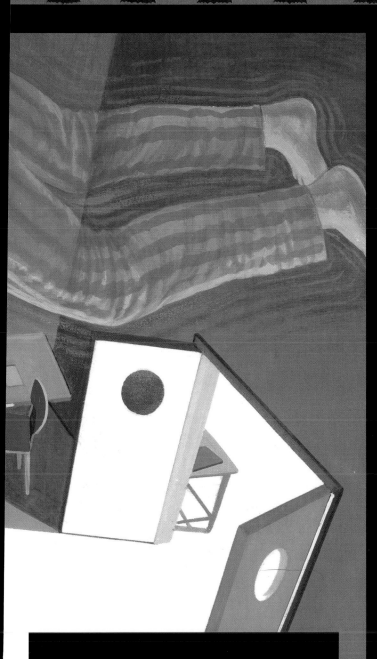

"The known is finite, the unknown infinite...we stand on an islet in the midst of an illimitable [endless] ocean of inexplicability [mystery]. Our business...is to reclaim a little more land."

T.H. Huxley (1825–1895), zoologist and writer

Today, people's psychic abilities and supernatural powers are often used commercially – dowsers look for oil and other precious minerals while hypnotism and mindreading are popular entertainment on TV and at the theater. Yet there are still a great many unexplained features of the world of the supernatural, and various mysterious powers and events that are beyond our control.

Thousands of people have described out-of-body (near-death) experiences (left), in which their spirit seems to float away from their body. Could this be what it is like to die? No one has yet found an explanation for this mysterious phenomenon. Religious miracles have been claimed for thousands of years, and are still said to occur today. While many incredible events, and amazing acts of healing can be explained, several continue to baffle scientists and investigators. Despite modern technology, we still have a great deal to learn...

Hi-Tech SPOOKS

Modern science is developing at a breathtaking speed. New technology enables us to explore and understand more about our world and our universe. Scientific techniques, like radiocarbon dating, help historians and archaeologists to unravel the mysteries of the past. Space laboratories, radiotelescopes, and space probes are constantly investigating the mysteries of the skies at close quarters. Satellites give scientists information about the atmosphere and the weather. As technology advances, we may discover new explanations for phenomena that we now consider supernatural.

Are the mind and the brain the same? Although many people believe that our thoughts and feelings are nothing more than the results of electrical and chemical changes, there do seem to be differences between the mind and the brain. When we dream, for example, our minds are not linked as closely to our bodies as when we are awake.

PROBING THE MIND

Some scientists believe that our thoughts are due to electrical and chemical charges in the brain, which they can monitor with an electroencephalograph (EEG) machine. This shows changes in brain activity at various times.

ALIEN CROP RAIDERS?

In the 1980s, strange circles began to appear in cornfields all over England. They were almost perfectly circular and the crops had been flattened without harm to the stalks. People said they were either made by aliens or the weather. High-tech gadgets have been used in attempts to recreate such circles, but without success.

PHOTOGRAPHING THE BEAST

Infrared film has been used in the tracking of several ferocious creatures which have terrorized sheep on British moors since the 1980s. Some witnesses describe huge black dogs. Others say there must be a new breed of wildcat or that big cats have escaped from wildlife parks. There are still many different theories about the strange beasts' identities.

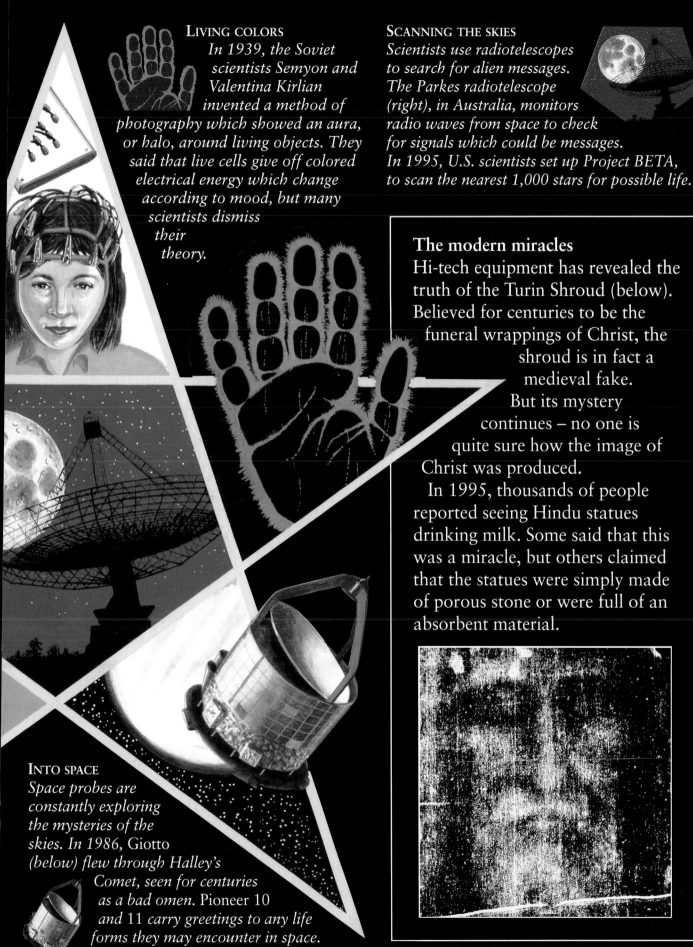

LIVING COLORS
In 1939, the Soviet scientists Semyon and Valentina Kirlian invented a method of photography which showed an aura, or halo, around living objects. They said that live cells give off colored electrical energy which change according to mood, but many scientists dismiss their theory.

SCANNING THE SKIES
Scientists use radiotelescopes to search for alien messages. The Parkes radiotelescope (right), in Australia, monitors radio waves from space to check for signals which could be messages. In 1995, U.S. scientists set up Project BETA, to scan the nearest 1,000 stars for possible life.

The modern miracles
Hi-tech equipment has revealed the truth of the Turin Shroud (below). Believed for centuries to be the funeral wrappings of Christ, the shroud is in fact a medieval fake. But its mystery continues – no one is quite sure how the image of Christ was produced.

In 1995, thousands of people reported seeing Hindu statues drinking milk. Some said that this was a miracle, but others claimed that the statues were simply made of porous stone or were full of an absorbent material.

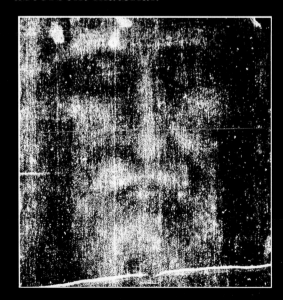

INTO SPACE
Space probes are constantly exploring the mysteries of the skies. In 1986, Giotto (below) flew through Halley's Comet, seen for centuries as a bad omen. Pioneer 10 and 11 carry greetings to any life forms they may encounter in space.

The Unsolved MYSTERIES

Some people think that modern science will never be able to help us to fully understand ourselves and our world. There is now a growing interest in strange phenomena and in new beliefs and powers, and there are a great number of occurrences that simply cannot be explained by reason alone. When we say things like "I can feel it in my bones" or "It's all in the stars," are we unconsciously talking about powers and memories that we all have, although we may not understand how they work or how to use them? Should we try to use these powers again, to help us in our daily life?

What is spontaneous human combustion? This is one of the most puzzling mysteries of the natural world, recorded for thousands of years. Its victims catch fire suddenly and for no obvious reason. The fire starts as a small flame on one part of the body, and does not appear to affect furniture or other objects near the victims.

IT'S RAINING FROGS AND FISH
Rains of frogs, toads, fish, stones, and ice have occurred throughout history. In 1911, an alligator fell from the clouds over Evansville, Indiana! Whirlwinds may suck up the objects, then drop them, but no one is sure.

A VISION OF THE FUTURE
Nostradamus (1503–1566) was a French astrologer. In his book Centuries (1555), he predicted events like the rise of Hitler, the Great Fire of London, and the end of the world – in 1999!

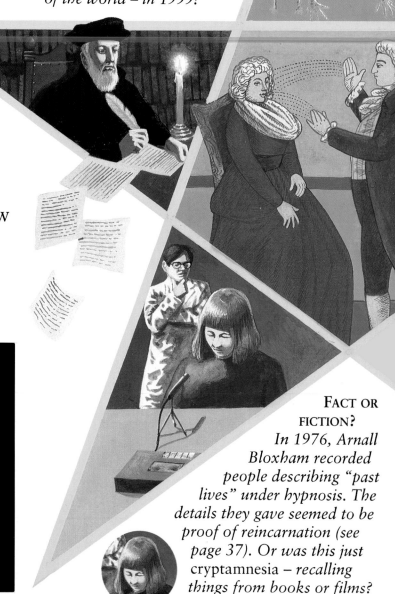

FACT OR FICTION?
In 1976, Arnall Bloxham recorded people describing "past lives" under hypnosis. The details they gave seemed to be proof of reincarnation (see page 37). Or was this just cryptamnesia – recalling things from books or films?

Who needs telephones?

Telepathy is when one person sends thoughts to another without speaking, writing, or using signals. It seems to be strongest between twins. Identical twins who have lived apart for many years sometimes find their lives have followed similar patterns. In the early 20th century, tests were conducted at the Psychical Institute of Japan into the power of thoughtography. Some psychics appeared to produce images and writing on sealed photographic plates, under laboratory conditions, just by the power of their thoughts, as in this European example.

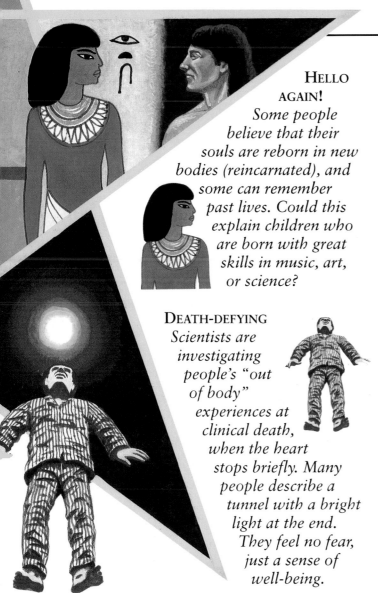

HELLO AGAIN!

Some people believe that their souls are reborn in new bodies (reincarnated), and some can remember past lives. Could this explain children who are born with great skills in music, art, or science?

LOOK INTO MY EYES

Hypnosis is a method of sending a patient into a trance then using the power of the mind to alter his or her mental or physical condition. There are even cases of painless surgery being carried out when the patient is under hypnosis, without the use of chemical anesthetics.

DEATH-DEFYING

Scientists are investigating people's "out of body" experiences at clinical death, when the heart stops briefly. Many people describe a tunnel with a bright light at the end. They feel no fear, just a sense of well-being.

Many mysteries to solve

Whatever we may believe, the supernatural touches all our lives. Science helps us to understand our earth and the universe, but people still search the skies for alien craft and scientists explore the world's last wildernesses. Perhaps, even in our high-tech age, we still want to believe in gods, monsters, spirits, and mysterious human powers.

TIME

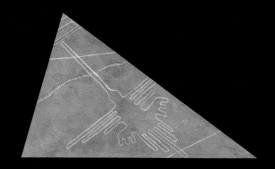

50,000 B.C. *First use of magic*
Before 10,000 B.C. *Stone Age peoples bury their dead weighted with stones to stop their ghosts from rising*
2800 B.C. *Stonehenge probably begun, on Salisbury Plain, England*
2300–2100 B.C. Epic of Gilgamesh *written on clay tablets*
c. **2000** B.C. *First known use of astrology, in Babylonia*
1950 B.C. *Crete flooded after huge volcanic eruption*
600–200 B.C. *First system of horoscopes invented*
A.D. **77** *Pliny records strange rain of frogs*
565 *Loch Ness Monster first seen*
900 *Christian Church declares that all types of magic are evil*
1000–1500 *Giant statues built on Easter Island, Pacific Ocean*
1555 *Nostradamus' Centuries*
1842 *"Feejee Mermaid" appears in Phineas T. Barnum's traveling show*
1862 *Sirius B discovered near Sirius*
1872 Mary Celeste *crew vanishes*
1890 *James G. Frazer writes* The Golden Bough, *describing two types of magic (homeopathic and contagious)*
1897 *Bram Stoker writes* Dracula
1910–1913 *Thoughtography tested at Psychical Institute, Japan*
1917 *"Fairy" photographs published*

LINE

1921 First
reported sighting of
Yeti, in Himalayas
1927 Ancient Nazca
lines and patterns across Peruvian desert discovered by light aircraft pilot
1934 First photo taken of Loch Ness Monster (later exposed as fake)
1939 Borley Rectory, world's most haunted house, destroyed;
Kirlian invents method of photographing auras of objects
1944 "Flying disk" invented and test-flown in Germany;
"Foo fighters" first seen, in Germany
1945 Five planes vanish in Bermuda Triangle
1947 "UFO" crash reported near
Roswell, NM, but quickly hushed up
1948 U.S. Air Force sets up
investigation into UFOs

1967 Erich von Däniken
writes Chariots of the Gods?
1972 Pioneer 10 launched,
carrying messages of greetings
1976 UFO incident over Iran;
Bloxham tapes suggest reincarnation
1980s Circles appear in cornfields;
"Beasts" reported on British moors
1986 Giotto probe flies through
Halley's Comet and takes photos
1988 Turin Shroud shown to
be medieval fake

1995 Roswell film;
Hindu statues
"drink" milk;
Project BETA

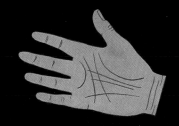

INDEX

PICTURE CREDITS
Abbreviations: t-top, b-bottom, r-right, l-left
4-5, 11tr, 19 both, 23, 25 & 37 - Fortean Picture Library. 11tl & 16 - Frank Spooner Pictures.
13 & 35 - Science Photo Library. 17 - Columbia Pictures (courtesy Kobal Collection)
29 & 31 - Hulton Deutsch Collection.